Growing in Love

3

Responsible to one another as members of Christ's body

PRINCIPAL PROGRAM CONSULTANTS
James J. DeBoy, Jr., MA
Toinette M. Eugene, PhD
Rev. Richard C. Sparks, CSP, PhD

CONSULTANTS

Sr. Jude Fitzpatrick, CHM
Pedagogy

Rev. Mark A. Ressler
Theology

Rev. Douglas O. Wathier
Theology

Daniel J. Bohle, MD (Obstetrics and Gynecology) and Anne Bohle, RN
Family Medicine and Parenting

REVIEWERS

Sr. Connie Carrigan, SSND
Religion Coordinator
Archdiocese of Miami
Miami, Florida

Mark Ciesielski
Associate Director, Office of
Continuing Christian Education
Diocese of Galveston-Houston
Houston, Texas

Margaret Vale DeBoy
Teacher
Arbutus Middle School
Arbutus, Maryland

Diane Dougherty
Director of Children's and
Family Catechesis
Archdiocese of Atlanta
Atlanta, Georgia

Harry J. Dudley, D. Min.
Associate Executive Director
of Faith Formation
Archdiocese of Indianapolis
Indianapolis, Indiana

Steven M. Ellair
Diocesan Consultant for
Elementary Catechesis
Archdiocese of Los Angeles
Los Angeles, California

Kirk Gaddy
Principal
St. Katharine Campus/
Queen of Peace School
Baltimore, Maryland

Connie McGhee
Principal
Most Holy Trinity School
San Jose, California

Barbara Minczewski
Religion Formation
Coordinator
Diocese of Davenport
Davenport, Iowa

Sr. Judy O'Brien, IHM
Rockville Centre, New York

Kenneth E. Ortega
Consultant for Media and
Curriculum
Diocese of Joliet
Joliet, Illinois

Sr. Barbara Scully, SUSC
Assistant Director of Religious
Education
Archdiocese of Boston
Randolph, Massachusetts

Rev. John H. West, STD
Theological Consultant,
Department of Education
Archdiocese of Detroit
Rector, St. John's Center for
Youth and Families
Plymouth, Michigan

Harcourt
Religion Publishers

Our Mission
The primary mission of Harcourt Religion Publishers is to provide the Catholic markets with the highest quality catechetical print and media resources. The content of these resources reflects the best insights of current theology, methodology, and pedagogical research. These resources are practical and easy to use, designed to meet expressed market needs, and written to reflect the teachings of the Catholic Church.

Photography Credits
Art Resource, NY: Erich Lessing: 24; Scala: 31; **Bridgeman Art Library:** *Christ Blessing the Children,* by G.E. Cook, 1875 (stained glass), Cricklade Church, Wiltshire, UK: 28; *Christ walking on the waves,* from an illuminated copy of *Meditations on the Life of Christ* by St. Bonaventure (1221-74), Italian, mid-14th century (parchment), Corpus Christi College, Oxford, UK: 41; *Madonna and Child,* 1996 (w/c), by Jeanne Spencer-Churchill (contemporary artist) Private Collection: 40, 45; **Gene Plaisted/The Crosiers:** 36; **Digital Imaging Group:** 4, 7, 9, 10, 11, 18, 23, 29, 35, 37, 43; **FPG International:** Jim Cummins: 11, 17; Edward Ozern: 23; Telegraph Colour Library: 28, 33; Anne-Marie Webber: 4; **Image Bank:** Steve Niedorf: 15; Philip M. Prosen: 22, 27; Steve Satushek: 12; **Jack Holtel:** 19, 30, 36, 37, 41; **Masterfile:** J. David Andrews: 34, 39; John de Visser: 5; Larry Williams: 16; **PhotoEdit:** Robert Brenner: 34; Myrleen Ferguson: 37; Nancy Sheehan: 13; Stephen McBrady: 36; **Abby Aldrich Rockefeller Folk Art Center, Williamsburg, VA:** 40; **Skjold Photographs:** 13; **The Stock Market:** Mug Shots: 25; **Tony Stone Images:** Stuart McClymont: 16, 21; Lori Adamski Peek: 6, 43; Frank Siteman: 18; **Superstock:** 28; **Bill Wittman:** 10, 15, 22

Cover
Photo by **Telegraph Colour Library/FPG International**
Illustration by **Lori Lohstoeter**

Printed in the United States of America

ISBN 0-15-950657-3

10 9 8 7 6 5 4 3

Growing in Love

3

Dear God our Father, thank you for your gifts to us. Dear Jesus, Son of God, help us appreciate the gifts we have received. Holy Spirit, teach us to use our gifts to help others. Amen.

Together in Love

What do you see when you look out a window? You might see the sun and sky. You might see people and plants. How are all of these things alike?

You know that God **created** the world from nothing. His **creation** includes everything we can see and everything we cannot see. All of the wonderful things God made are signs of his love for us.

As part of God's creation, people are also signs of his love. God wants us to appreciate and enjoy other people.

All people are created in **God's image.** There are people of different colors, sizes, and ages. Even though there are many differences between people, every person can show us something about God. We show others what God is like when we love.

When we live together as a family, learn together as a group, or celebrate special times with others, we share God's love. We live out his plan for us.

Reflecting God's Image

God gives each person special gifts, or talents. There are many kinds of gifts. Some people draw well. Others can run fast. No one can do everything well.

Everyone has strengths and weaknesses. We can use our special gifts to help others who don't have certain gifts. And others can help us with things we don't do well. God wants us to become the best persons we can be. How can you use your gifts to show God's love?

Scripture
Signpost

God created man
in his image, in
the divine image
he created him;
male and female
he created them.

(Genesis 1:27)

One gift God gives us makes us different from
each other. We are created **male** or **female**, man or
woman, boy or girl. As mother or father, husband
or wife, brother or sister, each person has a special
part in God's plan for creation.

All people share some of the same gifts from
God. We all have the ability to think and love and
the freedom to choose. With God's grace we can use
these gifts well. We all need many of the same
things, too—food, clean air, and safe homes. It is
up to us to share God's gifts with our families,
friends, and classmates.

Gifts from God

List some special gifts that God has given you to share with others.

Some of them are plants, animals, love, people, the sea and food.

HomeLink For Your Family

We shared this chapter. _____

We have these questions or comments:

How do we see God?

Praise the Lord, all you works of the Lord, for God commanded and you were created! Praise the Lord, all men and women, girls and boys! Praise God's holy name!

(based on Psalm 148:1, 5, 12–13)

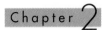

Chapter 2

Dear God our Father, thank you for the gift of feelings. Lord Jesus Christ, you showed us how to use our feelings to honor God. Holy Spirit, help us share our feelings and grow closer to God through prayer. Amen.

God Within Us

How do you know when someone loves you? What signs do you look for? How do you show your love for others?

We can see God's love everywhere. His love is present in all of creation, including our family and friends. His love is present deep within us.

Family members love each other and help one another. They spend time together. Family members share with one another and try to understand each other.

We can see love in action at school, too. You can show that you love your classmates by helping them learn and by letting them help you. You can show love by getting along with others.

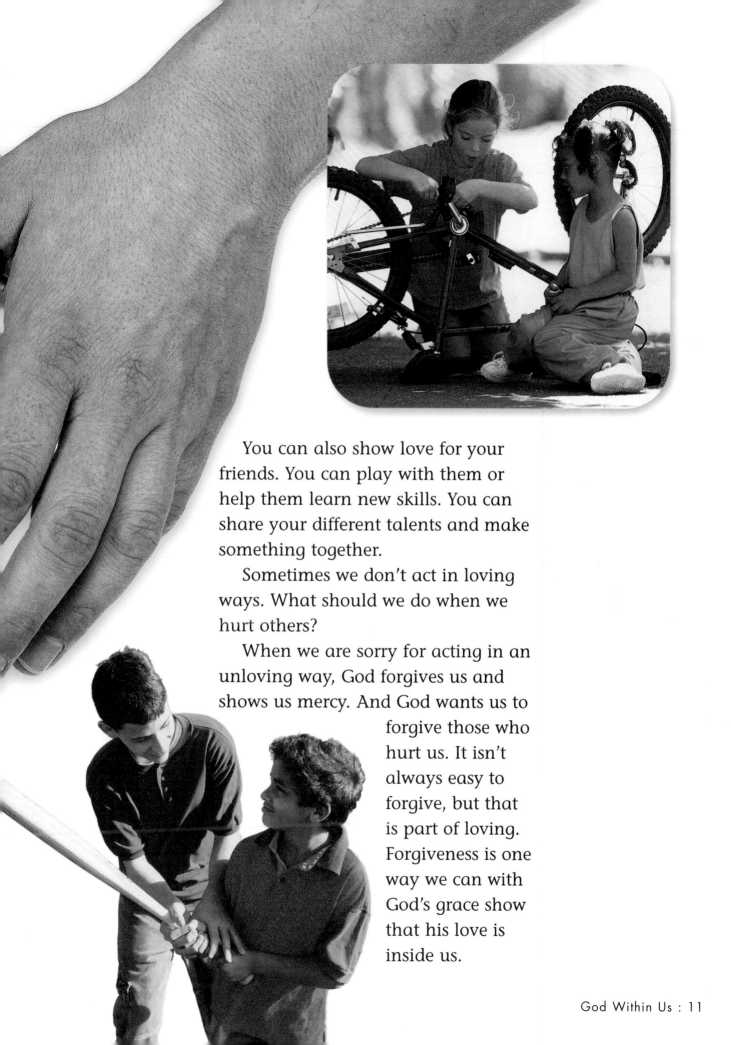

You can also show love for your friends. You can play with them or help them learn new skills. You can share your different talents and make something together.

Sometimes we don't act in loving ways. What should we do when we hurt others?

When we are sorry for acting in an unloving way, God forgives us and shows us mercy. And God wants us to forgive those who hurt us. It isn't always easy to forgive, but that is part of loving. Forgiveness is one way we can with God's grace show that his love is inside us.

Feeling God's Love

God has also given us **feelings.** In themselves, feelings are neither good nor bad. Our feelings help us understand ourselves and others. For example, feelings help us know when someone loves us and when we love someone.

But what about uncomfortable feelings? Even feelings that are unpleasant can teach us about ourselves and the world. Sometimes feeling afraid warns us about danger. Feeling that something is unfair might make us want to change what we think is wrong.

We can use our feelings to help people or to hurt people. God wants us to use our feelings to do what is right and good.

Sometimes you might need to talk with someone about your feelings. You can talk with your family and friends. And you can talk with God.

Stepping **Stones**

Prayer

Prayer is one way of talking to or being with God. We can talk with him the same way we would talk to a friend. Here are some suggestions for praying.

- Talk to God from your heart.

- Use your own words to tell God how you feel.

- Pray anytime and anywhere.

- Remember, God is always with you. He is your best friend.

Time with God

Write a letter to God about your feelings.

Dear God,

Sometimes I feel _____

_____ when _____

_____

_____

_____.

Love,

_____

HomeLink For Your Family

We shared this chapter. _____
We have these questions or comments:

_____

_____

_____

God be in my head, and in my thinking;

God be in my eyes, and in my seeing;

God be in my mouth, and in my speaking;

God be in my heart, and in my feeling;

God be in my hands and feet, and

in my doing.

(based on an old English prayer)

Chapter 3

Dear God our Father, thank you for our selves.

Dear Jesus, our Savior, teach us how to show love as you did.

Holy Spirit, help us show respect for our bodies. Amen.

Whole
Persons

What is a person? We believe that every person is created by God as a union of body and soul.

You know about your body and the wonderful ways you can use it to learn, play, enjoy yourself, and show your feelings. But you are more than your body. You are also your **soul**. Whether you are male or female, your body and soul together make you who you are. Humans are **physical** (body) and **spiritual** (soul) at the same time.

Everyone needs to learn how to live as a whole person. Body, mind, feelings, and spirit are all good gifts. We are called to use these gifts wisely and well.

Jesus, the Son of God, shows us how to live as truly whole persons. Jesus is fully God and fully human. In everything Jesus did, he showed God's love.

Showing Love

We show God's love when we respect ourselves and others. One way we respect ourselves is by showing **modesty** in how we dress, act, and speak. Modesty reminds us that some parts of our bodies are **private**.

One of the most important ways we use our bodies is to show love. Physical signs of love, such as hugging and kissing, can be very good. Modesty helps us decide when and how to show love.

Some physical signs are right at some times but wrong at other times. A husband and wife may show love for each other in physical ways that would be wrong for those who are not married. It is very wrong for an adult to use physical signs of married love with a child.

Catholics Believe

The virtue of modesty helps us show respect for our bodies. Modesty helps us show respect for others, too.

(See Catechism, #2521.)

Some physical actions are never good. Slapping, pinching, or biting are not signs of love. These touches can hurt. Hurtful touches are always wrong. Any touch that does not show respect for ourselves or others is wrong.

Not all people show respect for God's gift of the body. Some people do things that are harmful to others. Learning how to stay safe is one way of showing respect for our bodies.

Stepping Stones

Staying Safe from Stranger Danger

Everyone should know what to do to avoid stranger danger. Here are three things you can do to stay safe.

1. Say no!

2. Run away!

3. Tell someone!

Good
Signs of Love

Complete the following sentences.

I respect my body when I _love, care for each_
other.

I respect others when I _share my snack._

O Lord, I give you thanks that I am wonderfully made. Wonderful are your works! You know me well, both soul and body. *(based on Psalm 139:14–15)*

Chapter 4

Dear God our Father, thank you for our community. Jesus, our Savior, you showed us how to share love with others. Holy Spirit, teach us to help each other grow in love. Amen.

Community of Love

God didn't create us to be alone. He wanted us to be with other people.

People live together in communities. A **community** is a group of people who share their ideas and interests. Members of a community work together to get projects done. They have social gatherings. And they help each other in times of sorrow and in times of joy.

Every community is different. The people in a community have a special reason for being together. Your school community helps you learn. Your religion class comes together to pray and learn about God. What other communities do you belong to?

Many communities and families have **traditions,** beliefs or habits that are passed from older members to younger members. A tradition could be a holiday celebration or an unusual food. A tradition could be sharing a hobby with your grandparents or working in the family business.

Traditions are good ways for members of a community or family to show love, help one another grow, and celebrate both what they have in common and what makes them unique.

Being Responsible

Catholics Believe

The family is the basis for society, the model for sharing life and love.

(See Catechism, #2207.)

In a family or other community, each person has a duty. We are **responsible** for certain jobs. We must do our jobs well or else we will let down the rest of the community.

For example, if your mother asks you to watch your younger brother or sister, you must pay attention so that he or she doesn't get hurt. Caring for a sibling is an important job, a big responsibility. As you grow, you will be given more and more responsibility.

The parable of the Good Samaritan shows us our responsibility to others.

People in the community are important to us. They teach us and help us develop our talents. Communities help keep us safe.

They give us a chance to share God's love.

The choices that we make can change our community. If we choose to do our jobs well, we can make the community better. If we choose to share, we can help the community. But we can also choose to be lazy or selfish. What would that do to the community?

Think about the Good Samaritan and how he helped the man who had been robbed. *(See Luke 10:29–37.)* How did he show that he was a responsible person?

Witness *Words*

It's not how much you do, but how much love you put into the action.

(Mother Teresa)

Love in Action

Make a collage of pictures and words that show people in a community helping one another.

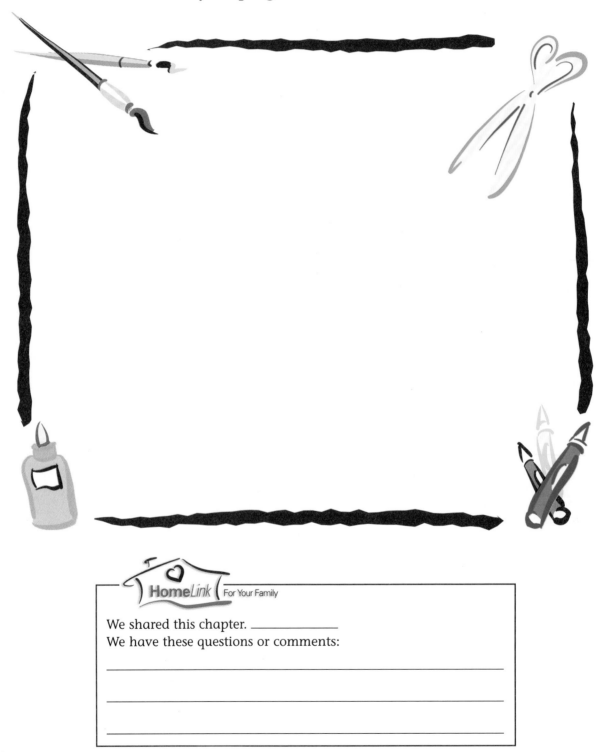

HomeLink For Your Family

We shared this chapter. _____
We have these questions or comments:

_____

_____

_____

We **thank you**, God our Father.

You made us to **love** you and **one another.**

Thank you for our **family** and **friends**

who share our **joys** and **sorrows.**

(based on Eucharistic Prayer III for Children)

Chapter 5

Dear God our Father, thank you for the ability to make choices. Dear Jesus, teach us how to make loving choices. Holy Spirit, help us show love when we make choices. Amen.

Loving Choices

Part of growing up is learning to make good choices. When you were small, you made a few choices for yourself. As you get older, you will make more and more decisions for yourself.

How do you learn to make good choices? Ever since you were young, your family has been guiding your choices. You have been learning rules and watching other people make choices.

Rules help us make good decisions and develop good habits. They help keep us safe. Rules bring order to communities.

People in **authority** lead and teach others. They make rules to help people live together and to help keep people safe. Sometimes members of a community make rules that are enforced by those in authority.

Parents and other caregivers have authority in a family. They have rules to guide their children to make good choices. Adult family members also teach by their example.

God helps us make good choices, too. Jesus has saved us and his example can guide us. Praying to the Holy Spirit can also help you make good decisions and give you the power to carry them out.

By making a habit of good choices, we develop **virtues.** Virtues can help us make the right choices in the future.

Making Things Right

Catholics Believe

The family is the first school of Christian love and forgiveness.

(See Catechism, #1657.)

Sometimes we do not make good choices. Maybe you chose to watch television instead of studying for a test. This could lead to a bad habit. Perhaps you called someone a bad name. You are not showing respect for that person. When we make a choice on purpose that hurts ourselves or other people, we **sin** against God.

What can you do after you have done something wrong? You can't change the action. But you can try to make things right again.

The Sacrament of **Reconciliation** is the most important way to make things right after we have sinned. To reconcile means to make peace. One part of this sacrament is thinking about our sinful choices and being sorry for them. Another part is asking God's forgiveness.

Why should anyone forgive us? God forgives us because he loves us. God's grace, his help and presence, is greater than the power of sin. Usually other people forgive us when they know we are sorry for hurting them.

Sometimes someone may not forgive us. But we shouldn't give up trying to love them. This should remind us to be willing to forgive others.

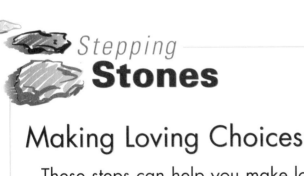

Dear Mrs. Von,
I'm sorry I stole from your store. I will pay you back when I get my allowance.
Jacob

Stepping **Stones**

Making Loving Choices

These steps can help you make loving choices.

- **Think about whether your choice will show that you love God and others.**

- **Think about whether your choice fits with how Jesus wants you to act.**

- **Think about whether your choice will help make you the kind of person you and your family can be proud of.**

- **Ask for advice from people you trust.**

- **Pray to the Holy Spirit for help.**

Living in Peace

Write down two actions that would help you live in peace with others.

mir   мире   Friede   vrede

fred

和

p _____

e _____

béke

a _____

p
a
c
e

c _____

e   malu, maluhia, la'i   paix

paz

HomeLink For Your Family

We shared this chapter. _____
We have these questions or comments:

_____

_____

_____

O Holy Spirit,
fill our hearts with
your love. Help us
choose what is right.

(based on a prayer to the Holy Spirit)

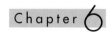

Dear God our Father, thank you for our families. Jesus, through the sacraments, guide us to live in love. Holy Spirit, help us live in peace with our families. Amen.

Family Life

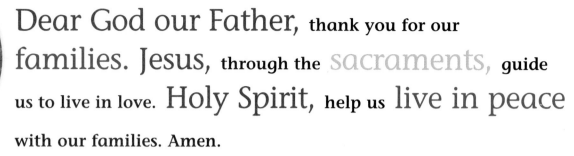

Life is full of change. Plants, animals, and people change. Families change, too.

A family starts when a man and a woman join in **marriage.** Husbands and wives want to share their love and God's love with children. Children come into families in several different ways.

When a husband and wife share in an act of married love, the woman can become **pregnant.** This means a baby starts to grow inside her. He or she is a new member of the family.

Sometimes a child becomes part of a new family when a parent remarries.

A child may be born to a woman who cannot raise him or her. That child is welcomed into another family through **adoption.**

Some adults become **foster parents.** This means that a child joins their family for a period of time. The child may stay with the family, return to the birth family, or join another family.

A new member brings joy and challenges to a family. God knows that, so he gives special love and grace to families.

Help from God

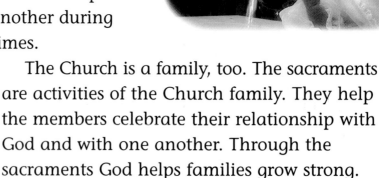

Christian families are life-giving.

(See Catechism, #1652–1654.)

Families are very important. Family members are special to one another. God wants them to teach one another about love. He wants them to celebrate good times together and help one another during bad times.

The Church is a family, too. The sacraments are activities of the Church family. They help the members celebrate their relationship with God and with one another. Through the sacraments God helps families grow strong.

When a woman and a man get married, they promise to love each other and live together for the rest of their lives. In the Sacrament of Matrimony, God's grace is given to the couple to strengthen their love and unity. The friends and family members at a wedding promise to help the married couple be faithful and **loyal.** Matrimony continually gives a man and a woman the grace needed to live out their vows.

Other sacraments help us all live in love as God's family.

A family celebrates when a new member joins it. The Church celebrates when a new member joins it, too. Baptism is the sacrament of new life in the Church. God welcomes each new member of the Church with special grace and love.

Families often share meals as a way of showing their togetherness. In the Church we share the Eucharist, the meal of God's family. Food makes our bodies strong. The Eucharist makes us stronger in virtue and unites us as God's family.

Sometimes family members say or do things that hurt other family members. Those members need to make up. Sin hurts our relationships with God and others. The grace of the Sacrament of Reconciliation helps us repair those relationships.

Every day, married people try to live out their promises to love and be loyal to each other. And every day, grace from the sacraments helps us show love and loyalty to our families.

Scripture
Signpost

Children, too, are a gift from the LORD, the fruit of the womb. . . .

(Psalm 127:3)

Love and Loyalty

Complete this story with an ending that shows love in action.

Phillipe was excited! His friend Jacob had asked him to play after school.

When Phillipe got home, his mother asked him to watch his little brother so she could nap, because she had worked all night.

Phillipe thought about Jacob. He thought about his mother. He thought about his brother. What could he do?

_____

_____

_____

_____

HomeLink **For Your Family**

We shared this chapter. _____

We have these questions or comments:

_____

_____

_____

God our Father,

through the waters of Baptism

you filled us with new life

as your very own children.

(based on the Blessing of Water)

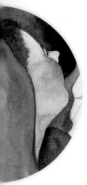

Chapter 7

Dear God our Father, thank you for trusting your people. Jesus, Son of God, thank you for showing us how to trust. Holy Spirit, help us be trustworthy. Amen.

People Who Trust

We know that God loves us. Because God loves us, we can **trust** him to be faithful to us.

God has always helped his people. His people trusted him in return. The Bible shows us that we can trust God to help us, too.

The story of Noah ends with a promise from God to his people. *(See Genesis 6:1—9:28.)* God promised that the whole world would never again be covered by a flood. He promised to always be there to help his faithful people in times of trouble. God sent a rainbow as a sign that we could trust him.

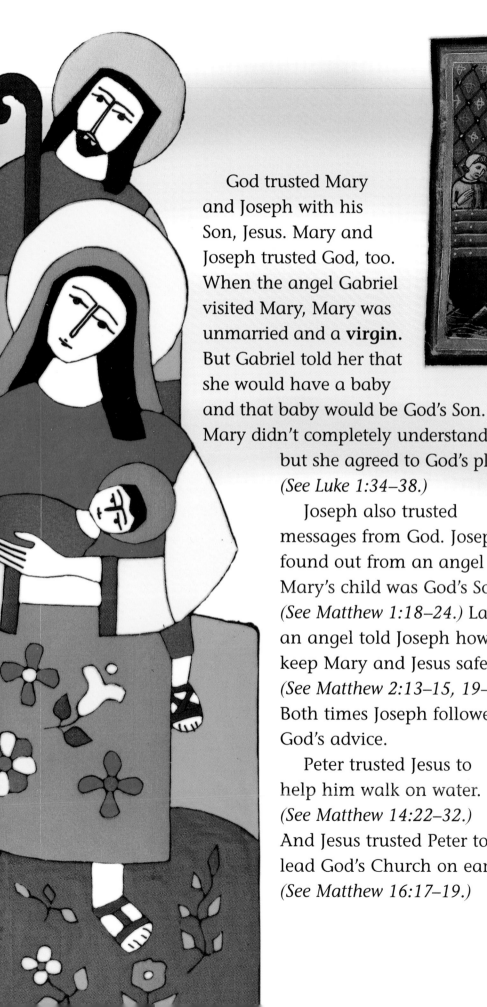

God trusted Mary and Joseph with his Son, Jesus. Mary and Joseph trusted God, too. When the angel Gabriel visited Mary, Mary was unmarried and a **virgin**. But Gabriel told her that she would have a baby and that baby would be God's Son. Mary didn't completely understand, but she agreed to God's plan. *(See Luke 1:34–38.)*

Joseph also trusted messages from God. Joseph found out from an angel that Mary's child was God's Son. *(See Matthew 1:18–24.)* Later an angel told Joseph how to keep Mary and Jesus safe. *(See Matthew 2:13–15, 19–23.)* Both times Joseph followed God's advice.

Peter trusted Jesus to help him walk on water. *(See Matthew 14:22–32.)* And Jesus trusted Peter to lead God's Church on earth. *(See Matthew 16:17–19.)*

Trust in Others

Catholics Believe

Mary is our mother because she trusted in God's plan.

(See Catechism, #968.)

Today, people still trust God. We know he will help us during hard times. And God continues to trust us. He trusts us to listen to him. He trusts us to love and honor him.

We need to trust people in our families, too. You trust your parents and other adult family members to give you good advice. You trust them to take good care of you.

Family members trust you in return. They trust you to study hard in school and do what they ask you to do. Family and friends trust you to be honest and keep your word.

What happens when trust is broken? People get hurt. They may become afraid to trust again.

There may be times when you break rules. Maybe you didn't call home when you were late. Your family may have been worried. But family members usually forgive each other. And each member of the family tries to be trustworthy.

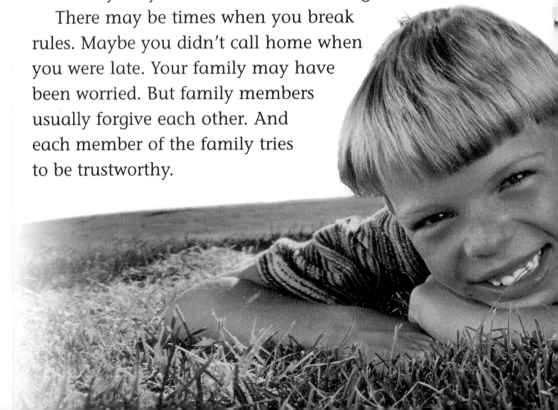

Trust is not always present in families. Without trust families can break apart. Relationships suffer and are damaged. If married people can't learn to trust each other again, they may get divorced. A divorce affects all members of a family, not just the married couple.

God always trusts us. We must always try to be worthy of his trust.

These parents trust the baby-sitter to take care of their children. What other people should a family be able to trust?

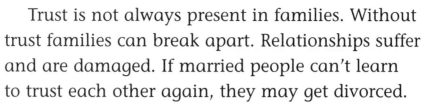

Witness Words

Here I learned by the grace of God that I should trust in the Lord, and all shall be well.

(Julian of Norwich)

Showing **Trust**

Draw a picture that shows an example of trust between family members.

HomeLink For Your Family

We shared this chapter. _____
We have these questions or comments:

_____

_____

_____

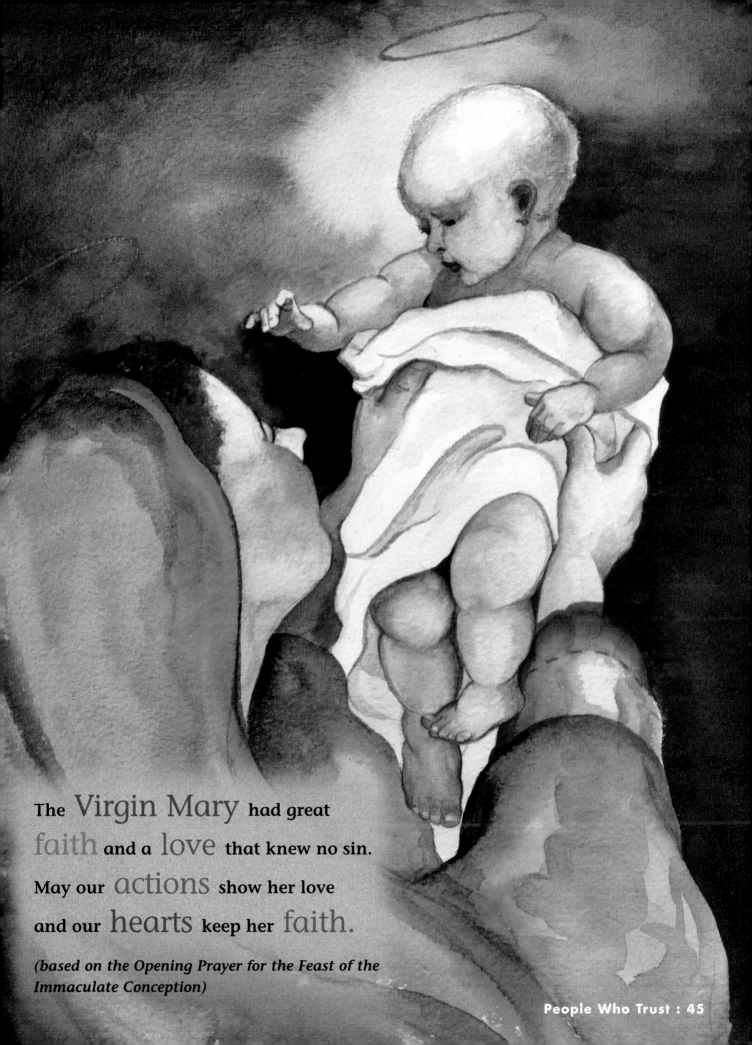

The Virgin Mary had great faith and a love that knew no sin. May our actions show her love and our hearts keep her faith.

(based on the Opening Prayer for the Feast of the Immaculate Conception)

Prayers and Resources

The Sign of the Cross

In the name of the Father,
and of the Son,
and of the Holy Spirit.
Amen.

The Lord's Prayer

Our Father, who art in heaven,
hallowed be thy name;
thy kingdom come;
thy will be done on earth as it is in heaven.
Give us this day our daily bread;
and forgive us our trespasses
as we forgive those who trespass against us;
and lead us not into temptation.
but deliver us from evil.
Amen.

Hail Mary

Hail, Mary, full of grace,
the Lord is with you!
Blessed are you among women,
and blessed is the fruit of your womb, Jesus.
Holy Mary, Mother of God,
pray for us sinners,
now and at the hour of our death.
Amen.

Glory to the Father (Doxology)

Glory to the Father, and to the Son, and to the Holy Spirit:
as it was in the beginning, is now, and will be for ever.
Amen.

Blessing Before Meals

Bless us, O Lord, and these your gifts
which we are about to receive from your goodness.
Through Christ our Lord.
Amen.

Thanksgiving After Meals

We give you thanks for all your gifts, almighty God,
living and reigning now and for ever.
Amen.

A Family Prayer

Lord our God, bless this household.
May we be blessed with health, goodness of heart,
gentleness, and the keeping of your law.
We give thanks to you,
Father, Son, and Holy Spirit,
now and for ever.
Amen.

The Great Commandment

"You shall love the Lord, your God, with all your heart, with all your being, with all your strength, and with all your mind, and your neighbor as yourself."
(Luke 10:27)

The Beatitudes

Blessed are the poor in spirit,
  for theirs is the kingdom of heaven.
Blessed are they who mourn,
  for they will be comforted.
Blessed are the meek,
  for they will inherit the land.
Blessed are they who hunger and thirst for
    righteousness,
  for they will be satisfied.
Blessed are the merciful,
  for they will be shown mercy.
Blessed are the clean of heart,
  for they will see God.
Blessed are the peacemakers,
  for they will be called children of God.
Blessed are they who are persecuted for the
    sake of righteousness,
  for theirs is the kingdom of heaven.
(Matthew 5:3–10)

The Ten Commandments

1. I am the Lord your God. You shall not have strange gods before me.
2. You shall not take the name of the Lord your God in vain.
3. Remember to keep holy the Lord's day.
4. Honor your father and your mother.
5. You shall not kill.
6. You shall not commit adultery.
7. You shall not steal.
8. You shall not bear false witness against your neighbor.
9. You shall not covet your neighbor's wife.
10. You shall not covet your neighbor's goods.